For enquiries, email: ***info.shiroberts26@yahoo.com***

Shirley Roberts

GN00730498

WHAT PEOPLE ARE SAYING ABOUT THIS BOOK

One of the best ways to build your self-worth is to accept who God has made you and the potentials He has deposited in you for the world. You are unique and special. No one is like you.

You are on this planet earth to discover your full potential, develop and deploy it to maximise destiny. However, you can't be able to do all these without knowing who you are. Knowing who you is the key that unlocks the world to you to display the glory of God in you. The glory of God can only be visible to everyone when you begin to take a journey to accept who you are and your assignment to accomplish.

What and who is stopping you from stepping into your calling, purpose?

Are you being stopped by self doubt?

If yes, then......

This book is written to empower you to regain your value and worth. This stops you from comparing yourself with others and evaluating yourself based on their validation and approvals of others about you.

Pastor Shirley Roberts, God bless you for birthing this great and insightful book for our generation. This is the book for this generation and the yet unborn.

Ferdinard Senyo Lawson BA Hons Public Health and Social Care.
Multiple Awards Wining Author.

By dipping into her life and taking you through a journey of deliverance this book really delivers. Encompassing a mixture of poetry, scripture and other powerful tools.
Shirley has managed to capture why transforming the mind is key to your freedom. Ask yourself today, "Stop, who are you hiding from?". Well done!

Marcia Richards

Very eye opening and enlightening. This book really does explain how your childhood can affect your thinking and way of life, however there is hope and key bits of wisdom scattered throughout the book to overcome past hurts and have a victorious future! I could not put the book down!!

Jessica Adekanmbi

Shirley has written a book that is thought-provoking, insightful, accessible and easy to read. It will be a great resource and help to many. Well done!

Ken Roberts

DEDICATION

To the Young Adults:
'You have a future'.

To the adults who are struggling with depression and fear:
'There is hope'.

To the Children of God who feels unworthy:
'There is grace'.

To the parents who fear making the same mistakes as their
parents:
'You can rise above'.

STOP! WHO ARE YOU HIDING FROM?

Table of Contents

Introduction

Walking through the corridors of life, you can encounter traumatic experiences, which leave long lasting scars upon your soul.

These become the signposts of memories, which, if you let them, influence your life forever. There are some agonising experiences we have encountered that have caused us so much suffering and these pains can feel like deep knife wounds, which seem to go on forever.

Hence, this has resulted in one hiding in a cave like a wounded bear. This deep pain has caused us to hide from interacting with others, to shy away and even distance ourselves from the rest of the world. We have even allowed our past hurts to dominate our lives and our future.

We live in a world full of hurt and pain. Every day is a struggle where our inner world is causing us to hide in our cave where we feel safe trying to live life constantly avoiding people. We are afraid of anyone getting too close. We find it difficult to talk or even open ourselves to reveal the real person crying in the background. We want to continue to keep up appearances or the lie that everything is picture perfect and yet our world is crumbling inside!

We do not know how to discuss the thoughts and struggles of the feelings we are facing inside, so we choose to bury the pain of the past and live in the shadows, isolating ourselves, which makes us live at a social distance on purpose!

There is a solution where you do not have to suffer in silence!

1

Setbacks in Life

From my experience, I know the feeling of being misplaced and overlooked. While dealing with brokenness, unforgiveness and shame; being misunderstood and thinking I needed to get away and escape from this world.

I was going through a complicated separation that led to an awful divorce after eight years of marriage. I suffered domestic and psychological abuse at the hand of my first husband. This was a great ordeal for me, as I knew that my separation would have to come out in the open, and this frightened me. Thoughts rushed through my mind of how people would judge me and treat me once they found out the truth.

I remember wanting to run away to America. Yes, it was that bad! But I had to stay in the United Kingdom because we had a daughter who needed stability, and I did not want to separate her from her father because she was too young to understand the circumstances.

Even though I needed support, I didn't want anyone to get too close to me. Conversations were difficult and even sometimes painful, especially when people tried to pry. Isolating myself seemed to be the best option at the time to protect myself and my daughter.

This unpleasant experience and abuse caused me to be wrapped up in my own emotional and mental prison. I was living under a dark cloud of self-doubt and low self-esteem, because of the constant oppression I suffered from my late husband. It was a living nightmare, from which I thought I could not escape. To God be the glory, my eyes were enlightened when I heard the encouraging words "Be yourself"! After months of praying and crying, I had the realisation that I needed to step out, take the mask off and just be myself.

I have discovered at the moment of birth; a seed of hope is planted into every one of us. These seeds drive us to reach our ambitions in life; however, setbacks in life can easily ruin or dilute this hope, preventing us from achieving our end goals or dreams.

We usually verbalise our hopes and dreams in early childhood, although it isn't until we are a little older that we realise that parents and other people close to us play a significant role in our lives which can either destroy our dreams or make them a reality.

Proverbs 13:12 says, "Hope deferred makes the heart sick, but a longing fulfilled is a tree of life."(NKJV) This means that when our hope is put off or postponed. We might feel that even God has forgotten us and is not interested in our condition.

Cycle of the Cave, Cage, and the Grave (CCG)

I am now going to take you through a journey of the 'Cycle of defeat', which operates daily in many lives, especially if you hide under your circumstances.

1. The Cave

The first stage is the cave. What is a cave? It is a natural underground chamber in a hillside or a cliff. It can be used as a place for temporary shelter, from the rain or even danger.

Let's consider a relevant example that many people face today, the fear of the unknown. In recent times the coronavirus disease (COVID-19) pandemic has spread across the entire world and has interrupted daily life as we know it. For example, employment rates have decreased, mental health and domestic violence have increased exponentially. The National Health Service (NHS) is overwhelmed and swamped with larger numbers of people. In consequence the lock down and restrictions have caused people to be self-isolated not only physically but also mentally.

It is not a surprise that many people are fearful, their minds going into overdrive, they have negative thoughts and fear the worst, such as losing their jobs or even their lives to the virus.

If we allow panic to take over our minds, it can drive us into a mental cave where fear suddenly creeps in and directs our thinking. We doubt our ability to cope in such a climate as the surrounding environment becomes more and more uncertain.

I can imagine thoughts of "What if I am made redundant?" Or "what if I contract the virus?," come to our minds, the list goes on. A part of us wants to believe the best, but the other part brings confusion and doubt. This leads us into double minded mindsets, so we can't see any way forward for our future. James says, "A double minded man is unstable in all of his ways". James 1:8. (NKJV).

Our emotions are immobilised; we cannot go forward or even make plans. Our fears speak to us. F-E-A-R grips our minds with False Evidence Appearing Real, Hence, I will chose to believe what the Bible says "But, God has not given us a spirit of fear, but a spirit of power and of love and a sound mind". 2Tim 1:7. (NKJV)

2. The Cage

The next stop is the cage: A Cage is a safe place or structure, where there are bars or wires in which birds or animals are confined, like a prison.

We can become trapped in a cage once we believe the narratives of our fears and rehearse them repeatedly. "What if I get the virus?", "What if I lose my job?", "What if I do not see my family again?". This causes us to self-isolate mentally and want to avoid socialising and interacting with others. Our home has now become our 'comfort zone', and we are too afraid to even leave our house.

Therefore, people who can discern us from the outside can detect that what was supposed to be a secure haven has now turned into a psychological cage. They can judge us based on our emotional state of your mind and then put a label on us. For example, they may label us as the person who is always afraid or someone who never takes risks in life.

We then become a victim of our emotions and circumstances, which becomes a self-imposed prison. For example, depression and isolation can lead one into substance or alcohol abuse as one tries to block out one's emotions. We make excuses to ourselves to stay quietly at home and have a drink. We can reassure ourselves by saying, "I am not hurting anyone". This could be our narrative to justify our actions in the cage.

Hence now you might wrestle with addiction, depression, fear, anxiety, isolation or any other negative conditions because of whatever circumstance you are in.

I want to encourage you that there is hope in Jesus Christ, only He can give you freedom from your addiction. Psalm 91:3 'Surely He shall deliver you from the snare of the fowler'.(NKJV)

3. The Grave

What is a grave? It is a hole dug in the ground to receive a coffin or a dead person.

Sometimes our cage can be turned into a grave, as we are slowly being buried alive, by our mindset and your inward chatter: such as "This is where I live, so there's no point in trying to change". "I have tried in the past and failed". "I feel defeated and disappointed and now. I have stopped trying for there is no hope!"

We have spoken negative confessions every day and those inward narratives are causing us to be buried alive slowly by depression, drug and alcohol abuse, bitterness, anger, and low self-esteem. The inner thoughts have taken over. Hence, we become who we say we are, our thoughts and words have created our world and who we have become today!

Words carry power; therefore, it is particularly important that we speak positive things over our life. We must learn to speak what to want to see, not how we feel.

I always remember that my circumstances can change, but I do not allow those circumstances of today to dictate my future.

I am encouraging you not to be buried under those labels that you or other people have tagged you with! It's time to stop hiding, come out of your comfort zone; addiction or situation and live the life you were born to live! Stop! Who are you hiding from?

As We Acknowledge The Inner Struggles:

I had to acknowledge my struggles and face the music inside, because I was like a broken record constantly playing the same tune every day in my mind and speaking it out loud and I was trapped in the cave, cage and grave.

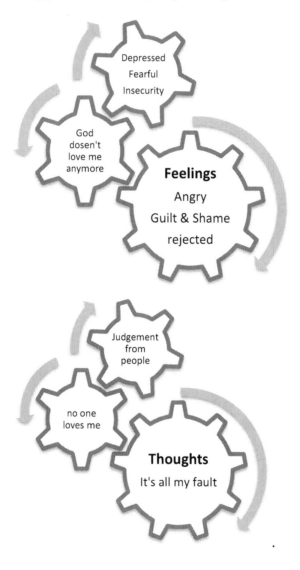

This first-hand experience of the 'CCG' process made me literally feel like I was buried alive with the thoughts and assumptions of what people were thinking about me. I believed the lies of Satan at the time; thinking no one would want to associate with me because of my past hurts and my past domestic and psychological abuse. I always felt ashamed or pitied by others. Whenever I went out, all these thoughts would flood my mind.

Being Real can be a Big Deal

God had inspired me to write the poem below concerning my feelings. It all gushed out onto the paper as I wrote about being real. This is one area some of us find it difficult to be honest with ourselves.

Being real can be such a big deal

"Being real can be such a big deal
Expressing how I really, really, really feel

Makes me feel nervous and knots inside
Struggling with heartaches and a mixture of pride
Want to say what's in the heart,

But making a fool of myself, and
Falling all apart.

Being frightened of rejection

Feeling, No!

Not again!

Then trying hard to keep my corner

And trying hard to defend.
So when you come along side me
I know I am on the mend".

By Shirley Roberts

Childhood Memories

Remember, your beginning is not such a bad thing. That you have experienced rejection, abuse or trauma in your childhood does not mean your life is over.

I am sure we all wish our lives were perfect, having a perfect home upbringing and having loving parents, who were not dysfunctional in their manner and conduct.

However, we have to deal with the cards we are dealt. In the real world, many people are unfortunately raised in dysfunctional homes.

Children can be rejected from birth where parents regret giving birth to them in the first place; probably because of their own sense of rejection, accompanied with all their traumas and fears of their past.

I remember being rejected by my parents after they had separated. We were all living together as one family unit one moment and the next moment, our parents abandoned my sister and me as teenagers at the ages of 12 and 13 years. All we knew was that our parents were going through a divorce and we had no say in the matter. Both our parents checked out and left us in the house by ourselves at that young age without gas or electricity. We had to fend for ourselves whilst still attending secondary school.

We were living in an abandoned house with no adult to protect or cover us from dangers as teenage girls. It was a terrifying time for me. My future was uncertain; I had no idea what was going to happen to me and my sister. So, I can fully relate to this scripture: *"Though my father and mother forsake me, the LORD will receive me" Psalm 27: 10 (NIV).*

While we were going through this devastating experience, we had to pretend to the outside world that everything was ok. Our parents told us to keep our lives private; hence, we didn't utter a word to a living soul. As sisters, we kept it to ourselves. No one knew we were home alone.

Under all the pretence, rejection was created and so were the emotional wounds. As teenagers, we had learnt to suffer in silence and sweep everything under the carpet. My mum told me from an early age not to share what was going on at home, so I grew up keeping secrets.

I learnt to pretend that everything was ok, even when it was not. Slowly, seeds of mistrust grew inside of me and the message was loud and clear: "Do not trust anyone". My parents constantly reminded us not to trust people. When I would leave home, they would say, "You can't trust anyone when you go out". Whenever we went out, they would say, "Remember, do not tell anyone your business!"

Childhood Rejection

To be rejected means to be cast aside or thrown away as having no value. To be rejected means being told 'I do not want you', 'you have no worth or value', 'You're not worth the food you eat' and 'you're not what I want'. When people are treated like this especially in childhood, like I was, it can be very traumatic. When a child experiences rejection, it can cause him or her to react negatively or unhealthy towards others. For instance, if someone tells you that they cannot make it to dinner or lunch as previously planned; you might take it personally as another rejection and flare up in anger. You might be labelled as a high maintenance person.

Remember, rejection comes to us all through normal situations. A person can be rejected during a job interview, from a football team or from taking part in competitions. In those instances, rejection should be taken calmly without getting into a tantrum.

Studies have proven that parents who had challenging upbringings themselves can have deep-seated emotions and unfortunately, transfer the hurt and pain to their own children.

Remember, 'Hurt People Hurt People' - Rick Warren.

Many people were raised by parents who unconsciously rejected their own children because they had a root of rejection in their own past. Unfortunately, they pass it on to their own children.

It's sad that many people do not know how to separate a person's personality from the person's actions. A child spills a glass of blackcurrant juice and the parents say, 'Bad girl' or 'Bad boy'. Sadly, the child believes automatically that he or she is a bad person. They cannot see that it is just the behaviour that is bad. The word 'bad' has been associated with who they are, rather than their actions.

The cause of rejection can startle; just a minor wound can open the door to rejection.
There are only very few people who are not affected by rejection by the time they are adults.

What are the causes of rejection?
Here is a non-exhaustive list of causes of rejection: Abuse, including physical, verbal, sexual, emotional and the withholding of love. Unwanted conception, contemplated or attempted abortion, a child born as the wrong sex (i.e. parents who wanted a boy but had a girl or parents who wanted a girl but had a boy), comparison to another sibling, adoption, abandonment, death of both parents, a parent with mental illness (the child may feel abandoned), peer rejection, turmoil within the home and marriage rejection, unfaithfulness or divorce. Since most of these reasons are common, most people are affected by rejection.

In the book, Creative Suffering[1] research was conducted on many of the world's greatest leaders. It was discovered that they all had one thing in common - they were all orphans. To his amazement, some of these super achievers had been victims of abuse and some were severely mistreated. About 75 percent of those who became celebrated achievers were estimated to have suffered serious emotional deprivation or hardship in childhood. Because they felt worthless inside, they would work themselves practically to death trying to have some value. As a result of that, many of them became successful.

In the book, *The Hidden Price of Greatness,*[2] we learn some powerful truths by looking at the backgrounds of certain individuals. The book explains how childhood suffering often sets the stage for a life of struggle. For example, American missionary David Brainerd became an orphan at the age of 14. This caused a significant loss of love and affection, which is so essential to a child's happiness. Some say David, like many orphaned and neglected children, might have felt an unusual burden of guilt, like he was responsible for his parents' death. He felt a great sense of rejection after being expelled from Yale for making a comment about one of his tutors. Even after

---

[1] Tournier, P (1983) Creative Suffering
[2] Beeson, R & Hunsider, RM (2000) The Hidden Price Of Greatness

apologising for the comment made, Brainerd was still dismissed from the University. He waged a constant fight against the disappointment over his expulsion. In April 1743, Brainerd began working as a missionary to the Native Americans, which he continued until late 1746. However, his illness from tuberculosis of the lungs prevented him from working. In his last years, he became immobilised by depression and had constant thoughts of suicide.

It is a sad lesson to learn what happened to David Brainerd. The book recorded that "by the 1700s, his greatest fear had come upon him". As a missionary, Brainerd died at 29. Even though he had a powerful ministry, he had become too sick to preach, teach or pray. The young man had exhausted himself trying to serve God with perfection. He spent himself so much that he became physically ill and died, because he felt so insecure from rejection. He did not give that area fully over to God. We all should learn not to exhaust ourselves in trying to be worth something. There is no use climbing the ladder of success at the expense of our health or our families.

We all truly need the love and acceptance of Christ. Rejection has no power over us because we are already accepted by Christ. Our worth and value does not come from us or what others think; it comes from God. We are valuable regardless of what happens because we are created in the image of God.

"You are of great worth in My eyes. You are honoured and I love you. I will give other men in your place. I will trade other people for your life." Isaiah 43:4 (NLV).

Traits of Childhood Trauma

There are some incidents that follow people into their adulthood. These incidents come because of childhood trauma.

- *I can't remember my childhood* - sometimes, a person may experience memory loss. Some people cannot remember their childhood. For some others, it is like a blur. Some do not remember occasions or even pinpoint moments of reflections of those memories. They try hard to think, but no thoughts spring to mind. It seems like a black hole.

- *I keep finding toxic relationships* – This is the inward narrative of 'We accept the love we think we deserve'. You find it difficult to hold a healthy relationship with someone who will love you wholeheartedly with no strings attached. You cannot trust people, so you go for detachable relationships, which are short-term. These are unhealthy relationships.

- ***I do not deserve love at all*** –Trauma follows avoiding loving relationships because you think you can't be loved at all. You cannot give or receive love. You lack emotional intimacy because of the fear of rejection. You feel too vulnerable to love, just in case you ruin it or worse, you get hurt.

- ***I am angry in a passive aggressive way*** – You have learnt from a young age that your needs are not important, so you make it a habit to suppress or bury your feelings. You learn to say to yourself, 'It doesn't matter', 'I can cope', though a slow hot pot is boiling up inside of you. This spills out in your relationships with friends, partners, or spouse. You are silently mad inside, but you say to yourself 'I am ok', 'there is no problem' and 'everything is fine'. You avoid letting people know exactly how you feel because you grew up avoiding straight forward talk and learnt to hide your genuine feelings.

- ***I keep hearing negative self-talk*** - Trauma makes a child think he or she will never be good enough. When parents constantly say negative things to their children, it demoralises the child and makes a person feel worthless. When parents speak these words to their children, especially in anger, the words become like stabs in the heart that cut, hurt, and impair them for life. These words are like darts and spears, cutting through your emotions and soul, causing wounds that will take time and love to heal.

These words pierce both ways - Your parents speak negative words over you and you internalise those words and speak those same words over yourself until they become your default settings!

- ***I am on an emotional roller coaster*** – You have mood swings; one minute you are sad and angry, the next minute you are happy and calm. Trauma can cause your emotions to be very unstable. This results in trouble making decisions. You act impulsively and have angry outbursts or frustrations which arise from nowhere. You become a difficult person and live like a pressure cooker; no one knowing when you are going to blow up.

- ***I do not know who I am*** – You feel like someone has stolen your identity because you cannot see who you are. You look in the mirror and you wonder who is staring back at you. You do not recognise yourself. You ask the question, 'Who am I'?

If you share any of these characteristics, you are reading the right book.

NOTE TO PARENTS – DO NOT OPERATE IN DEFAULT SETTINGS

The following three points were the template I used when I was raising my children. I wanted to ensure I did not make the mistakes my parents made. I had to renew my mind, change my thinking and go alongside the word of God.

"Don't copy the behaviour and customs of this world, but let God transform you into a new person by changing the way you think. Then you will learn to know God's will for you, which is good and pleasing and perfect." Romans 12: 2. (NLT).

1. **Do not operate in your default settings**

What is a default setting? A classic example is the computer.

A computer produced from the manufacturer has default settings already placed in its internal hard drive. However, we must change the settings for the computer to run a certain way. As individuals, I believe we all have a default setting on how to parent our children. This default setting comes directly from our parents.

Therefore, we have to be mindful of not repeating the same inappropriate behaviours we learnt from our parents and passing them down to our children. Remember, behaviours are caught and not taught. It is not what we say, it's how we act. You cannot say to a child stop swearing and punish him or her for doing so if you also use those swear words all the time.

I know growing up; my parents taught me the best way they could - with some good and bad values. They tried their best in the knowledge they had. Their mindsets were if we had food to eat, a roof over our head and clothes on our back that was enough. They did not consider our psychological needs. They could not express their love to us as children. They did not tell us they were proud of us.

They were not interested in our personal or our emotional wellbeing. They were just satisfied with our outer appearance.

"The Lord does not look at the things man looks at. Man looks at the outward appearance, but the Lord looks at the heart." 1 Samuel 16:7 (NIV).

Hence, the questions you should ask yourself are how often do you tell your children how much you love them or how proud you are of them? Do you reward them for good grades or good behaviours? Are you interested in what is happening in their world? Are you their friends and their parents? Do you have a good enough relationship with them? Are they able to express their genuine feelings? No matter how hard it is to hear their opinions of your own actions towards them, are you patient and pay attention to what they have to say? Also, do you respond in a calm and understanding manner, so they know they have a voice?

This makes it easier for them to express themselves later in life, rather than constantly being a victim to others.

2. Correcting your children, correctly

In disciplining our children, we have to be careful not to discipline out of anger or frustration. For example, my daughter had stepped on my toe. It was extremely painful and out of my pain and frustration. I told her, "Wait till you get home. You are in big trouble". She tried to explain and cried out, "It was an accident mummy". However, on my way home from the park, the Lord said, "Do not smack your daughter out of your anger and frustration". "Leave her alone. It was an accident".

Fathers do not provoke your children to anger, lest they be discouraged. Colossians 3:21 (KJV).

I made sure I did not repeat the words my parents spoke consistently to me, over my daughter. I refused to say she was stupid, not good for anything, not worth the food she ate (which was what my dad said to me and my sister). I could not afford to follow in their footsteps if I wanted my daughter to grow up as a healthy and stable individual.

3. Learn to instruct your children with love

From the time my daughter was in my womb, I had spoken the word of God over her. *I will praise you.*

For I am fearfully and wonderfully made; marvellous are your works. Psalm 139:14 (NKJV). I would say, I love her very much and God loves her with an everlasting love. I would say that she is fearfully and wonderfully made, I would tell her she was destined for greatness; I said she would achieve great things.

I would encourage her and read the Bible, and I helped her to memorise the book of Proverbs from two years old. I would write the scriptures on paper and stick them on the wall with blue tack. It turned into a game, where we had fun learning, reading, and memorising the scriptures together. *Proverbs 3:1-4.*

I taught her the commandments, how to pray and how to have faith in God; she became a Christian from the age of four. I prayed for her friends at the Primary and the secondary schools where she attended. I encouraged her to be a person of her word. I prayed I would be a godly example as a parent. Therefore, her default setting would be different and be Christlike.

CHAPTER

What is Love?

B elow is a poem I wrote about love, when I was pondering on the concept of love and what it meant to me.

What Is Love?

"Love is more than a feeling

Love is more than wheeling and dealing

Love is more than a mouse

Love can be strong as a house

As small seeds that grow where there are no boundaries

Love is when you are not expecting to get, but you are expecting to give.

Give! Your time, care and attention to the one you love.

Find out how they tick
Not withholding oneself, but being free to be yourself
Love is like a garden, where beautiful flowers grow
They can be inspired by the love that is shown
Love comes with butterflies, which trigger joy and
Excitement inside, which reminds you
You're alive!
The beauty of being in love is not contained in time or space
Love is constant, it never dies

You cannot kill or bury it no matter how you try"

By Shirley Roberts

What's Love Got To Do With It?

Children naturally idolise their parents and look up to them. In a child's eye, the parent is always right. So, it is difficult for children to understand why their parents do not love them naturally. That is why when a parent is abusive towards a child, rejecting and depriving them emotionally, the child takes the blame.

To gain some love and attention, the child will act either extra good or awfully bad. The destructive nature of a dysfunctional parent to child relationship has a detrimental and a distorted effect on the child, especially when it concerns the expression of love to themselves and others.

When children are growing up knowing that their parents do not love them, it causes them to feel unworthy. Then the child expresses their inner narrative of, "I am not good enough". Or "It's my fault".

These same children become adults thinking they are unlovable. As a result, they look for love in all the wrong places. Unfortunately, this causes more damage and creates self-doubt and insecurity which ultimately opens the door for more abuse and rejection. And the cycle continues.

However, there is a beautiful description of love found in the Songs of Solomon. Love is described in strong terms.
"For love is as strong as death, its jealousy as enduring as the grave. Love flashes like fire." Songs of Solomon 8:6 (NLT).
In these words, we hear such a powerful passion flowing out. In the Greek language, there are four different words for 'love'.

1. **Eros**: This is sexual love from which we get the word 'erotic'. This represents physical love which flames with passion between a man and a woman.

2. **Philia:** This is the love between friends and equals. It is a genuine love from friendship with feelings for people you connect with for years. This gives room for receiving support and encouragement.

3. **Storge:** This has to do with love of family - a genuine love of parents to children or among siblings and treating each other with authentic love and respect.

4. **Agape:** This is God's kind of love; it is divine love that exists despite the conditions. This love continues to shine because it is unconditional. Here, someone gives love without asking or expecting anything in return. God has this kind of love towards us. This is the type of love we need to have for humanity. This love is unselfish towards people. This love gives and keeps on giving!

It is a type of love which is not based on emotions or feelings. It's based on choice. This kind of love says, 'I choose to love despite what you have done to me. I will love despite the pain'. *"For God so loved the world that He gave His one and only son, that whoever believes in Him shall not perish but have eternal life". John 3:16,(NIV).*

Hence, we can consider the statement that God is love! When we love, our love can run out; but God's love is stable and constant. It doesn't die and we can't kill it, no matter how hard we try.

In the film, 'The Cross and the Switchblade', there was a preacher called David Wilkerson who went to New York to bring the message of salvation to street gangs. David was speaking to Nicky Cruz about the message of Jesus. Nicky Cruz wanted to cut David with a switchblade and in the film, David said, 'You can cut me into bits with the blade, but all the pieces in me will say 'Jesus loves you'. That was a profound statement which got me thinking about God's love towards us and how He loved me. *Film- The Cross and the Switchblade* [3].

Looking for Love

It is funny how the search for love can be an urgent adventure in life. The giving and receiving of love are some of the highest and purest expressions of our humanity.

However, this search for love is sometimes unfruitful; too often, loneliness is the unspoken reality of many. Whether it is feeling lonely within a crowd or simply the everyday loneliness we experience from time to time, many individuals experience this.

A lot of us do not like the thought of being alone or the prospect of being lonely. We might wear the best masks, but

---

[3] The Cross and the Switchblade, June 1970, USA. David Wilkerson.

behind the façade is the fear of being left out and being denied affirmation and affection. Feeling lonely is scary.

Can you remember some of your childhood or teenage experiences where love went wrong? These experiences can drive us back to our caves; however, sometimes our willingness to take risks is controlled by the deep hurt within.

The question is, can we find someone who will genuinely love us and let us love them in return?
Love is a strong natural desire we all feel and yearn for, so much so it is expressed in countless movies, songs, and poems; like the one I wrote at the beginning of this chapter. We want to reach out to the world, but our desires can come with difficult emotional attachments.

Finding love in the right places is difficult. The idea of love is often better imagined and at times, we need to work hard to find a secure and comfortable place for both parties where there is mutual love and respect.

In the beginning of a new relationship, there is fun and excitement. Being in love is beautiful and comes with excitement that light up our lives. During courtship, there are flowers, chocolates, candlelight dinners and the niceties attached to young relationships. You and your beloved accept each other and share affection and intimacy with each other. All these cause hope and dreams to blossom. When you find genuine love, it brings balance into your life.

Although human love is beautiful, it cannot compare to the love that Jesus showed mankind when He died on the cross for all our sins. Let me emphasise the word 'all'! Jesus accepts everyone - no matter your race, social status, past, or mistakes. Only Jesus can love us 100 percent as we are. Only God's love is unconditional and helps us to regain our self-worth. Only God can forgive us, befriend us, and give us eternal life. This is a gift He gives to us all, if we will accept it.

Just Love Yourself

Learning to love yourself can be difficult, especially when you weren't shown how to. One perfect avenue of learning how to love yourself is from a loving home environment. But if you lived most of your life believing that you were worthless or unlovable, it will be hard to love yourself truly.

I would say you need to remind yourself; you are fearfully and wonderfully made as you look at yourself everyday in the mirror. You need to learn to appreciate yourself.

Self-love can provide you with self-confidence or self-worth and it can cause you to feel positive in going about your everyday business.

When you learn to love yourself, you will take care of yourself by being concerned about your physical and mental wellbeing. In taking exercise and watching what you eat also making sure you rest and sleep when required.

Decide to love yourself and learn to be content and thankful for what you have. This can help you to stop complaining about yourself to others and stop you worrying about what other people think.

Practical Ideas For Loving Yourself

1. **Love your own company:** Do something fun or pleasing for you alone to enjoy. Learn to value your time with you. Start reading books or enrol on a course to expand your knowledge. Watch movies or programmes of interest or just go for a walk in the park to be inspired.

2. **Learn to forgive yourself for your mistakes:** Learn to consider your mistakes, where you can decide to forgive and forget. Be willing to learn from them.

Also love yourself despite the wrong doings you have done in the past.

3. **Treat yourself:** Buy yourself a bunch of flowers or your favourite box of chocolates. Get out of your comfort zone and try new ideas or adventures.

4. **Start a Journal:** Learn to write down your thoughts and feelings. You can look back to see how to cope with future situations. This can help you to centre on the positives to get rid of negative experiences so you can focus on the good things and not the bad.

5. **Make a vision board:** Visualising your goals, which will help you to be motivated and excited about your future. You can focus on your dreams and start to love your life and yourself.

Remember, God is love, and He shows His love to us. The best example of learning how to love ourselves and others is from God. *"A second is equally important; 'Love your neighbour as yourself." Matthew 22:39. (NLT)*

If we want to learn how to love ourselves or others, the Bible's teachings must guide us on love by showing mutual respect. Be kind to one another, preferring one another. He reminded us to treat all people in the same way, the law should not be a 'respecter' of persons or we would be breaking the' Royal law'. Love shows no favourites of persons. If one breaks this law in any point, then he has broken the whole law. James 2:8-13

What is the Royal law? James referred to the 'Royal Law' which is the commandments of loving thy neighbour as thyself.

4

Relationships

Below is a poem I wrote on healthy relationships.

Relationships

"Relationship is a virtue

Relationship is a trust

Relationship is a covering

For its within God we trust

For He is our foundation

He is our true guide

We cannot take for granted

Or gather hidden pride

Whether it be the parent, spouse or

Whether it be the friend
You must stand united, so you will never be divided again

Always strive to forgive at any given time
For it is in Him we trust, and in Him we believe
That He will keep our relationships fresh

With every prayer we breathe."

By Shirley Roberts

Toxic *Relationships*

A toxic relationship is characterised by unhealthy behaviours, especially when one partner is undermined, not supported and abused in all ways. Toxic relationships involve partners who are emotionally and physically damaging to the other partner.

While healthy relationships encourage one's self-esteem or emotional needs, toxic relationships damage self-worth and drain energy. Healthy relationships show care, respect, compassion and interest in one's partners' welfare and growth.

A relationship should be a safe place where one can be oneself without fear. It should be a place where one is comfortable and secure.

A toxic relationship is unsafe and destructive, filled with temper tantrums or fits of rage, insecurity, jealousy, intimidation, manipulation, self-centeredness, dominance and control with complete dysfunction.

Toxic relationships are not limited to just those between spouses, but can be between parents and their children, between friends, teachers and students, mentors and mentees, co-workers or business partners. 4

Signs of toxic relationships:

- **Avoiders** – These people suddenly become inaccessible, so they play the avoidance game. They are always making excuses for lateness in meeting you: "I had to work late ', 'An emergency has arisen'. They always limit their exposure to you. For no tangible reason, they withhold care and support.

---

4 www.healthscopemag.com Toxic Relationships; What they are and 8 Types in Health Scope
By Thomas L. Cory, Ph. D.

- **Dumpers** - These people throw you into difficult situations to let you stumble. They make you feel insecure and can ruin any confidence you have or are trying to build. This causes more trauma, which leaves you petrified. A typical example is in a class where a lecturer puts a student on the spot in front of the entire class, intending to embarrass or humiliate the student. They put others in awkward situations. To them, it is a psychological game.

- **Blockers** – These people avoid meeting your needs by out-right refusal of your requests. For instance, you ask them to meet you and they bluntly refuse. Or they withhold information that can advance you. They enjoy having a sense of dominion, power, and control over you. The aim is to stop you from developing your skills and abilities.

- **Destroyers / Critics** – The destroyers tear you down and undermine your actions in subtle ways. Whereas, the critics use belittling tactics that are far more overt. They often tear you down publicly, especially in front of people you know. Studies suggest that some critics may be unaware of the impact of their volatile behaviour. *(Darling 1986).*[5]

Co-dependency - Whose life are you living?

Sharon, a consultant at *everydayhealth.com* says that "Signs of co-dependency include excessive caretaking, controlling and preoccupation, with people and things outside ourselves".[6]

The question is, do you feed off constantly being a hero to others, or do you devote all your energy to other people more than to yourself? If yes, you could be co-dependent.

You might also be co-dependent if your feelings of happiness are associated with another person's happiness other than your own. Therefore, you hide behind other people.

There might be cases where you feel you cannot express yourself because you see yourself as worthless. Instead of looking to yourself, you look to others and worry about them instead. You put others' needs before your own.

---

[5] "What to do about Toxic Mentors" The Mentoring Dimension: The Journal of Nursing Administration, Maypp.43-44.
[6] Everydayhealth.com – signs of Co-dependency by Sharon Wegscheider-Cruse

That is why you can have someone being totally committed to a partner who has an addiction to alcohol, substances, or food; and solely takes care of the partner, forgetting about his / her own personal needs. Such people will be willing to handle those partners for years, while their own lives are diminishing.

Signs of co-dependent behaviour:

There are some signs that cannot be missed which point to the fact that a person is co-dependent.

- You find it difficult to decide in a relationship. You always want the other person to decide on behalf of both of you. You lack the capacity to make up your own mind.

- There is a problem in expressing yourself. You find it difficult to discuss how you feel or even express your feelings. You literally shut down when you are asked how you feel.

- There is an impressive display of a lack of trust in your own judgment. You have low self-esteem issues so you think other people's judgments are sounder than yours. You do not think you are capable of making good decisions because of disappointments in your life.

- You are overwhelmed by many fears such as fear of rejection, being alone; fear of embarking on projects because of the thought of something going wrong and your lack of confidence in yourself but value for other people's opinions in preference to your own.

These behavioural patterns can be detrimental to you and people in relationship with you. This unhealthy behaviour can cause a lot of grief and be burdensome, especially to someone who genuinely loves you. It can be exhausting to deal with a person who has lived like this for a long period.

Remember, your worth and value should not be tied to someone else. Your worth and value should be found in yourself so you can be a blessing to yourself and others around you.

Some Practical Solutions To Adhere To:

- **Assess the relationship** by looking at the recurring patterns of behaviour in your current and past relationships. Be honest with yourself.
- **Recognise healthy support** as it does not mean your relationship is doomed, but it will need more work to get things on track. It is vital

to learn healthy life skills to enable you develop non-co-dependent relationships. You can ask for help from a trusted friend, doctor, counsellor, and continuously re-evaluate your support network.

- **Set boundaries for yourself and ask yourself a series of questions, such as;**
  1. Why am I doing this?
  2. Do I have to help, or do I feel I have to help?
  3. Will this drain any of my resources?
  4. Try to offer suggestions or advice when asked, rather than constantly intervening, and making people's minds up for them. Step back and let them make their own decisions.
- **Stop the pattern** by reminding yourself that you can only control yourself. You have a responsibility to manage your own behaviour and reactions. You are not responsible for your partner's behaviour or anyone else. Try to discuss workable solutions with them, rather than for them.

- **Practice valuing yourself.** Co-dependency and low self-esteem are often linked. If you link your self-worth to your ability to care for others, it can be devastating when those relationships end.

Spend time with people who treat you well. Surround yourself with positive people who value you and offer acceptance and support. Limit your time with people who drain your energy and say or do things that make you feel bad about yourself.

Do things you enjoy, take up hobbies or other interests. Set time to do things that make you happy, whether it is going to the gym, reading a book or even going for a walk. Take care of your health, care for your body and guard your general and emotional wellbeing. Eat the right foods and sleep regularly.

- **Let go of negative self-talk**. If you criticise yourself, the challenge is to stop those negative thought patterns. Start telling yourself positive affirmations and confessions.

Be Intentional & Fight

Below is a poem based on fighting for your life.

Be intentional and fight

"A soldier's life is not an easy one
He must always be prepared!
On his guard with his gun

He cannot afford to be afraid at any time or day
For if the enemy knows this
He can be blown away
As soldiers of God we are called to fight
To be aware of the battle and always unite

As Winston Churchill said many years ago,

"We shall fight on the beaches; we will fight as we go".
We must always be vigilant to watch and pray
Teach our fingers to war and not to play
For the enemy is fierce, and we should not give in

So the battle is fierce, for us to live in
For with Christ on our side
We know we win!"

By Shirley Roberts

Stop Believing Negative Results

I concluded that I need not believe the lies or the seeds that were planted in me as a child, like "You are no good, you are worthless, loser, waste of space and idle good for nothing".

All those negative words had left me wounded and traumatised. The memories of words and the mistreatment were being played in my mind repeatedly like arrows, cutting into my emotions and soul. I kept feeling sorry for myself and would constantly say, "why me". I would internalise these thoughts for years, from the time I can remember.

However, I know I do not have to believe those words anymore. Today is a new day, and it is time to stop believing all those words that were thrown at you as a child and the way you were treated; being rejected or abused. I decided it is time to stop.

I came to the revelation that God understands all your grief and sorrows. He took on everything imaginable from bad to horrific behaviour; he took it all upon the cross. He was wounded for us and bruised for us, so that we can be healed. *Isaiah 53:4-5 (NLT).*

I knew I didn't have to be bullied by my fears anymore. I was thinking about the Batman Begins[7], where the scarecrow character made a gas which when released into the atmosphere caused people's worst fears to manifest in their minds. It reminded me of what I mentioned fear is False Evidence Appearing Real.

I had to deal with my fears. What are the fears dominating and manifesting in your life? Is it fear of the future, fear of the past, fear of making mistakes, fear about marriage and will your relationship last, fear of studying or fear of driving; the list can be endless.

---

[7] Film (2005) DC Comics

Ellen Biros, explained that, "co-dependent behaviours are typically rooted in childhood upbringing".[8] Some fears are identified in life by patterns you learn from your parents and repeat in your own future relationships and this usually keeping playing repeatedly, until you put a stop to them.

Let me explain: When you think about having children, it can be scary if you have come from a background of neglect and abuse or one whose parents had serious behavioural flaws. This can cause you to doubt whether you will make a good parent. Fears seep into your mind like 'Will I make a good parent', 'Am I competent enough', 'Am I worthy', 'Or am I qualified to carry out this role', - It can be very daunting!

Every time I remembered my childhood, I decided that my relationship with my own children will be different. I wanted to raise my children differently from how I was raised. I decided I will make a conscious effort to be interested in my children's wellbeing because I desired to have a great relationship with them. I wanted them to open up to me and be honest with me. I wanted them to see me as a friend, rather than just a parent. I can say that God has granted me that relationship with my daughter.

---

[8] Ellen Biros, Licensed Clinical social worker in USA

Steps to overcome fear and break free from the chains of the past

- **Use your mouth to proclaim what the word of God has to say about fear.** We are reminded from the Bible that when fear comes, we can declare: *"There is no fear in love. But perfect love drives out fear."* 1 John 4:18 (NIV).
  "For God has not given us a spirit of fear, but of power and of love and of a sound mind." 2 Timothy 1:7 (NKJV)

- **Be honest to God and speak to him about your fears.** The Lord cares about you and your problems. If you come to Him in prayer, He will hear and deliver you. He says you should *"Give all your worries and cares to God, for He cares about you".* 1 Peter 5:7 (NIV).

- **To fully let go of the past, we need to forgive those who have wronged us.** What did Jesus say on the cross about his attackers? *'Father, forgive them; for they do not know what they are doing '.Luke 23:34.(NIV).*

The question is why did Jesus say "Father, forgive them"? Jesus represented the Father on earth to us. He is our example of how to operate in forgiveness! The last action on the cross is for us to learn to 'FORGIVE'. Forgiveness is the key to breakthroughs and healing. This is how we break the chains of Satan off our lives.

We must remember to forgive and not harden our hearts; instead, we must release our hearts into the hands of Jesus because His love is unconditional towards us. We can close the door to the enemy and let Jesus strengthen our heart and mind with the power of the cross. *"Forgive us our sins; for we also forgive everyone who sins against us". Luke 11:4 (NIV)*

We must repent so that God can forgive us. We have no right to hold someone else in unforgiveness when God has forgiven us completely. Therefore, the Bible talks about forgiving 7x77 times over. Jesus said to him, "I do not say to you, up to seven times, but up to seventy times seven". Matthew 18:22 (NKJV).

Many of us are living with the brokenness inside that we are hiding from the outside world. We do not know how to relate with others due to our experiences. Some of us are still caged by the feelings that we were robbed of something special or precious - the dignity and the essence of self-respect within our inner being. It is like we have been robbed of how to love ourselves in balanced ways, let alone knowing how to love someone else.

How many of us can draw from the memories of our dysfunctional families, alcoholism, violence, drug abuse, domestic abuse, are always at the back of our minds. These experiences leave wounds that cut through our hearts. We are walking around like broken vessels. Even God can relate to a broken vessel, as it is mentioned in the Bible, explaining how a person can feel. *"I am forgotten like a dead man, out of mind: I am like a broken vessel."' Psalm 31:12(NKJV)*

The question is, do you want to receive healing? If so, are you ready and willing to do what is necessary to receive it?
He heals the broken-hearted and bandages their wounds. Psalm 147:3 (NLT)

Stop The Comparison Trap

We need to stop ourselves from pursuing the idea that everyone is better than we are and believing the narrative that our self-worth and value are less than our parents, partners, siblings, or friends.

However, we should learn to look at our own value through our talents and abilities. Look at what God has naturally blessed you with and start having a heart of gratitude and thanksgiving for all the good things in your life.

I started focusing on my strengths instead of majoring on my weaknesses. I was determined to gain a degree in Fashion even though my mum had no confidence in me passing. I studied despite her dismay and passed with flying colours. I saw God's hand moving in my achievements in life. I remembered passing my driving test and jumping up for joy, like I had won a million pounds. I recalled at work; the men mostly would make fun of me as a learner driver. I would have my driving lessons at lunch time. I did not care because I knew in my heart, I had already passed my driving test.

Start realigning yourself with your hidden childhood dreams that were stolen from you through toxic relationships I always wanted to get a degree and as soon as I was out of the toxic relationship with my first husband, I started my degree course and completed it with honours in Business.

Furthermore, you need to learn to say you are enough and you need not compare yourself with others as a measuring stick. *2 Corinthians 10:12 (NIV)*
Be encouraged; we were all created as originals and God made us individuals and not photocopies of someone else. So, remember we are independent and should not live as a co-dependent person, living someone else's life. God has a plan and purpose for each one of us. You might have experienced a traumatic experience as a child where a parent died and left

you alone and you might be blaming yourself that you were not enough for that parent to live.

Today, I am encouraging you. You are enough! Stop believing the lies in your mind, you are sufficient, and you need to speak those words of affirmation over yourself daily until they become a reality.

Fight For Honesty

Being honest can be a good problem because sometimes we have to break the cage of denial. We can either block out the message of truth because of our emotions, or we can reinforce the cage to serve as a pain barrier.

I found being honest was the greatest hurdle I had to encounter dealing with all the pain and rejection that was going on inside me. I had to be honest with my childhood; I could not keep it as a secret anymore. My cage was broken when I did that first step, and then all the other situations that had occurred came flooding out. The auto pilot default setting was broken. I realised I had the permission to speak as I spoke to my counsellor about what I had experienced in my first marriage. A liberty and freedom came, and I was more able to tear down the negative thought patterns.

I believe God wants us to be honest to ourselves and honest with him. That why He requires us to have truth in the inwards parts. *Psalm 51:6 (NIV)*

This was when David repented of his sin. It took David nine months before he repented, after Nathan, the prophet, spoke to him and pointed out his sin. He wrote a prayer of repentance of acknowledging his wrongdoing. *'Create in me a clean heart, O God and renew a right spirit within me' Psalm 51:10 (KJV).*

Naomi recognising her bitterness and rejecting Ruth

I was thinking about, *Ruth 1:20*. When Naomi announced, "Do not call me, Naomi."

She told them, "Call me Mara, because the Almighty has made my life bitter". Naomi was honest with her condition where she was suffering inside, feeling God had rejected her because her husband and two sons had died. She was consumed with grief, self-pity, and regret. She even felt isolation, where she wanted her daughters-in-law to go away. However, Ruth stayed with Naomi; eventually went back to her hometown; Bethlehem. She knew everyone received the news of her husband and sons dying. She could not hide from the town, and God allowed Naomi and Ruth to be accepted and loved.

Naomi's name means pleasant, and Mara means sad and bitter. Naomi wanted to be called sad and bitter. How many times do we want to be called by a situation which is not permanent? Being called by your situation can cause you to believe you will always stay in that condition.

The woman known by her condition - 'with the issue of blood'

There was a woman with an issue of blood; she was bleeding continuously for twelve years. Some say she had a rare bleeding disorder called haemophilia, or she had a continual period. This woman was well known for her condition. She was rejected by society because she was considered as unclean by the Levitical law; no-one could touch this woman; no one could even hug her (like with social distancing today). She had spent all her money on trying to get a cure. Imagine all her savings were gone; she was at the end of her resources and she had suffered many things from many physicians. This had gone on for twelve years and she had spent all she had, and she was not better, but grew worse.

Hope came when she heard about Jesus, her mind set had changed, her inward chatter; her narrative became intentional when she made the statement; *"If only I may touch His clothes, I shall be made well". Mark 5:25-29. (NKJV)* The Bible says immediately the fountain of blood was dried up, and she felt in her body that she was healed of the affliction.

Fight Against Your Accusers

What does accuse mean? 'To be charge with a short coming or error; blame or to bring charges against someone for a crime of offence'.[9]

The main accusers we fight against in our minds are guilt and shame. Let us examine this more closely. The meaning of guilt; is when you have done something wrong and you have a feeling of remorse. So, with the loss of integrity, you are trying to forget the wrong. People can act in this way to distract people by operating in a self-destructive behaviour because of the fear of man or the thought of what people will think of you now?

However, when shame is displayed in public; you feel embarrassed or unworthy if you were to confess the action or behaviour. So, we do not want people to see this side of us. So, we are fearful of the consequences and feel ashamed, so we want to hide because we do not want anyone to know. *Psalm 38:2-11.(NKJ).*

---

[9] Readers Digest Universal Dictionary (1987)

Guilt is an emotion you feel, and it affects your self-worth and value system, which conveys your heart and inside your inner world that you have done wrong. *Psalm 32:1-5.(NLT)*.

However, shame can say, "I am the mistake" and it can make you as the individual feel worthless and depressed. It can cause you to hide away from people or even go into isolation, for fear of rejection.

I found an interesting insight when I was considering the word contempt; a feeling of being worthless. The question why people harbour contempt of themselves is because it helps them as an individual to gain power and to protect themselves from their own emotions of guilt and shame. So, they keep people from getting too close, so they will not discover their shame-based behaviour. Isolation is the key; you decide to make statements in your mind;
"I do not need anyone; I am better off alone". Therefore, pride can enter in to harden one's heart, so you will not come out of your world of guilt and shame.

I was reading the story of the woman caught in adultery. She had to deal with guilt and shame in front of the crowds of people. This was a powerful account of how Jesus showed forgiveness. The women had committed the sin of adultery, but Jesus said, *"He who is without sin cast the first stone"*.

The men who wanted to stone her, but they could not. By Jesus asking, 'who is without sin to throw the first stone'? He had dealt with the woman's accusers.

I could imagine the woman was feeling fearful, with the sentence of death hanging over her head. But Jesus challenged the accusers by starting to write on the ground. Each man from the oldest to the youngest dropped their stones. They all knew they had committed sins in their own lives.

My husband usually says, "Everybody is guilty of something, so before we judge others, let's look into our own past". *Ken Roberts.*

How did Jesus deal with her guilt? He forgave her and told her to go and sin no more. Also, how did Jesus release her from shame; he asked, *"Where are your accusers?"* Also, he asked her the question, *"Didn't even one of them condemn you?"* She replied, "No, Lord". And Jesus, replied, "Neither do I. Go and sin no more." *John 8:1-11.(NLT).*

This is a powerful illustration of taking away guilt and dealing with the consequences of shame.

The Unconscious Moments Of Thought:

Feedback of the Johari Window

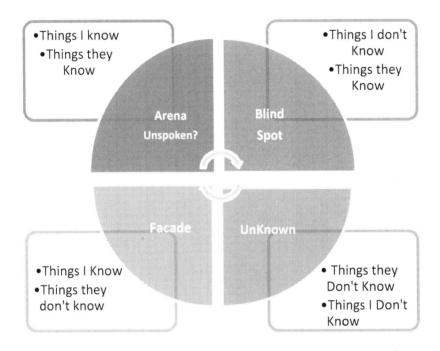

'The Johari Window' by Joseph Luft and Harry Ingham in 1955.

The Johari window has four quadrants that represent four combinations:

1. *Open Space: Known to you – Known to others.*

This is what we know about ourselves from our outer appearances and others can see how we act and what we look like.

2. **Blind Spot: Unknown to yourself – Known to others.**

Our blind spot is what we do not see about ourselves. However, we unconsciously give hints, but only to the discerning person. They pick up our body language, hidden suggestions, or sarcastic terms. We might say 'I am only joking', yet the word of God says that out of the abundance of the heart, the mouth speaks. *Luke 6:45.(KJV)*.

3. **Hidden Area: Known to you – Unknown to others.**

The things you know about yourself, but you put on an act or facade to others. Where people wear masks, I am happy, but sad; I have no money to buy shopping. I am unhappy with my job, etc.

4. **Unknown Area: Unknown to yourself – Unknown to others.**

This is the area of discovery; Where the Holy Spirit plays a prominent part to go into the roots of your life, your childhood, your basic thoughts and assumptions about yourself and your relationship with God. The hidden areas where your mind is a blur. Only God can reveal the areas that are hidden to you. However, to the discerning, God can reveal those areas to them as well. Only God knows the secret things, and only He can reveal areas in your life you do not understand. But by His Holy Spirit, it will no longer be a mystery to you. The reason I chose this model, is to prove man can create models to understand the workings of how a man thinks and behaves. However we have to receive the revelation from God, by the Holy Spirit, who has the final word or the upper hand in knowing the secret things of our lives and areas we do not understand or do not remember from our childhood. So, we need to humble ourselves and seek our God to find out what to do.

God knows everyone and sees everything. He is the one who created us in the inward parts. He is the one who gave us our DNA.

Fight Against Offence

David was a man after God's own heart. When he sinned, he confessed to God *Psalm 51:6-7*. David was inspired by the Holy Spirit to write the Psalms, so we can be inspired and encouraged today!

Be honest to God and ask Him to purge you. Ask Him for a heart transplant. Like David, he asked God to create a clean heart and renew a right spirit within him. We can ask God for a new heart, so we can do the will of God.

The greatest attack we all can hold easily is offence. The Bible says offence will come. When it comes, it hinders our relationships in general and our relationship with God, in particular. Therefore, offence needs to be dealt with daily.

Whenever offence comes, we have a choice as to how we respond. We can choose to walk in forgiveness or unforgiveness.

Let us look at the steps of offence:

The Offence

What is offence? 'The act of causing anger, resentment or displeasure or to take offence; to become, angered, displeased or resentful: feel hurt.'[10]

- *Choose your reaction*:
- Yes/No
- If you choose yes – you hold onto the offence – walk in unforgiveness
- If you choose no - you let go of the offence - walk in forgiveness

---

[10] Readers Digest Universal Dictionary (1987)

The offence invites its family members: Offence brings in: unforgiveness, bitterness, pride, strife, and division.

When these attitudes settle in our lives a stronghold is created. So, no-one can get to you. You become wrapped up like an Egyptian mummy and start decaying within yourself. The only word that can break that stronghold is repentance. It breaks the walls of the offended.

Unforgiveness can bring fear in, not wanting to confront an issue. The temptation is to sweep it under the carpet or avoid the person. Also, you will consider if you forgive that individual, they will get away with that misdeed. If you hold on to their offence, you would not be free. So, the Bible encourages us to deal with the offence quickly and swiftly, or the offence will deal with us.

Remember, an offended person sees things differently from a forgiving person.

Offence can be a distraction in life. It keeps us from a position of victory and causes a break in your relationship with your father God and others.

When offence comes, it can cause us to see life in a different light, which is distorted, corrupt and in deceptive. Your ears will receive corrupt and deceiving information.

A Comparison in Attitudes:

Offended Person	Forgiving Person
Deception	Truth
Distortion	Insight
Corruptible	Incorruptible
Misunderstanding	Wisdom with clarity
Division	Unity

When offences come, we need to guard our hearts. The gospel of *Matthew chapter 5* gives us instructions on how to deal with offences.

A woman's story about Offence

A lady was sharing with me, she had so many hurts and emotional wounds that made her keep her distance from everyone. She lived an isolated life such that she would not go to certain places because certain people who had hurt her were there!

Through this, she opened the door to the enemy by holding on to the offence which brought in unforgiveness, pride and deception, then isolation and fear. This spirit kept her trapped for five years. She had allowed the enemy to keep her in that state for years. She just could not forgive the person who had broken her heart. Therefore, she was in a stronghold.

However, she talked to God about her problem. She had a dream where she was clearing out the rubbish in her home. They were black bags. These were the hurts she had accumulated in her life. They had built up over the five years. Coincidentally, the next day, she received a CD in the post on forgiveness.

She realised that over the years, she had a root of bitterness inside of her. This was clouding her judgment in everything she was doing. She repented and forgave the person and others that had hurt her. This brought her great deliverance and freed her from the emotional cage she was in.

Unforgiveness causes hurt to spread. When one person hurts you and you do not forgive them, you automatically will not forgive the next person who offends you. And this snowballs into an enormous mass of unforgiveness that generates into bitterness.

Therefore, the offence can cause blind spots, like the 'Johari Window'. We do not see our blind spots and we cannot see the attitudes we hold, but others can see them, so like David we have to go to God and pray. '*Search me, O God, and know my heart; test me and know my concerns. See if there is any offensive way in me; lead me in the way everlasting'. Psalm 139:23-24(KJV)*

We cannot receive the full love of God ourselves, when we are harbouring unforgiveness towards ourselves and others. We cannot forgive ourselves for what we have done in the past and it is eating us up inside. We cannot even say I am fearfully and wonderfully made, and God loves me, we cannot accept his love, because we are rejecting his love instead.

CHAPTER 6

A Bridge to Life

I wrote this poem when I had to make a choice for change.

A BRIDGE TO LIFE

"Life can be looked upon as a bridge
The hurdles in life can become gateways into destiny

The bridge of life can make you or break you

BUT!

That is, if you let it!

Courage can come from a make or break situation, where
you have a choice.
Whether to sink or swim

Conquer or fall
Take a stand or give in

Which one?

It is up to you

You choose!"

By Shirley Roberts

Break Free From The 'CCG'

Remember the CCG model we mentioned in the earlier part of this book – The Cage, Cave and Grave? We agreed that if not properly addressed, it could lead to intense feelings of rejection and negativity. We said that it was important to break free from the CCG and move ahead with life.

Fortunately, influential people in history have been trapped in this rut but broke free at last and made progress. Let us observe some famous people who suffered from mental health issues and problems. They made a choice to go forward despite their conditions. They moved on with their lives.

- *Vincent Van Gogh*- *He was a great artist in the 19th century. He* suffered from temporal lobe epilepsy as well as other mental and physical conditions.

- **Winston Churchill** – He was a War Prime Minister during the Second World War He was well known for his epic speeches. He was open about his 'black dog' which was the name he gave his periodic dark and depressive moods.
  He was noted for saying, "Success is not final; failure is not fatal: It is the courage to continue that counts."

- *Abraham Lincoln* – *He was the 16th President of the United State of America.* He faced many tragic situations. His sweetheart died and his heart was broken. He suffered from a nervous breakdown and was bed-ridden for six months. He endured constant failure and six defeats in elections and politics. However, eventually without giving up he became the President.

- *Florence Nightingale* – She was a nurse of the Crimean War. She was known as the Lady with the lamp. She was a writer. She established St. Thomas Hospital in London, England. She suffered from Bipolar disorder, having highs and lows. She heard voices and experienced severe depression.

- **Sheila Walsh-** She is an Author and Bible Teacher. She had a nervous breakdown. Her book 'Honestly' takes you through her journey out of depression.

All these individuals contributed a great deal to the world and history despite their inner struggles and conditions. This should give us all great hope for the future.

Change Your Mindset

We all have a choice on how we live and conduct ourselves. When we come to a crossroads in life, it is time to make a choice on how to make progress.

Some of us need to look at how we are living and recognise that God is speaking to you from this book. God is giving you a lifeline to make a fresh start, a new hope, and a new way forward.

It is up to you to make a choice! Whose report will you believe? Are you going to continue to entertain negative thoughts about yourself and continue to speak out the negative words which attract negative situations? Or will you speak words of life and wholeness to yourself? Remember, *"Death and life are in the power of the tongue, and those who love it will eat its fruit." Proverbs 18:21 (NIV)*.

Therefore, our negative thinking and negative speaking will cause a negative outcome. You will have what you say.

Many people are overly concerned about what others think, say, or do. They are so focused on 'they'.

According to the dictionary, 'they' represent 'people' or 'the third person in a case'.

The enemy is always speaking lies to you to discourage you. And he does this through 'they'. One day, God revealed who 'they' are.

T- Thoughts
H – Hiding
E – Enemy (the)
Y- You (in)

Meaning he can place thoughts into our minds which are negative, and we have a choice whether to believe or reject them. For instance, he can whisper negative thoughts such as

'Do not bother trying to apply for that job because they will not accept you', 'you're not good enough', 'no one will love you', 'you are ugly', 'you are too old', 'you are too poor', 'it's not possible to buy that house' and the negative thoughts go on and on. The devil puts fears and stumbling blocks in our minds to make us doubt ourselves. Also the sentence of what will they think.

However, we now know the devil paints a false picture with our fears (False Evidence Appearing Real) to make us doubt the integrity of God's word. He promotes the thoughts that God is not there, and God does not love us. He spreads his lies to make us doubt God. But we are encouraged with this scripture: *"God is not a man that he should lie, does He speak and then not act? Does He promise and not fulfil?" Numbers 23:19 (NIV)*

God's thoughts are higher than our thoughts, and His ways are higher than our ways. He formed us all in our mother's wombs. He knew all our characters who we were going to become. God knows the end from the beginning. He knows our past and future.

"For I know the thoughts that I think towards you', says the Lord, 'thoughts of peace and not of evil, to give you a future and a hope." Jeremiah 29:11.(NKJ). (Isaiah 55:8 & Jeremiah 1:4,5)(NKJ).

- *Forgiveness is Key*

  Forgiveness is the key to letting go and breaking through from the Cave, the Cage and the Grave. You need to decide intentionally to consciously and deliberately release yourself from feelings of hurt, anger and resentment towards any person or group who has harmed you, regardless of whether they deserve your forgiveness.

- **Process of forgiveness**

  First, admit the injury and acknowledge the harm or wrongdoing. Tell your story to someone who is a doctor, counsellor, Pastor, Christian support team or someone you trust. Be led into a prayer for forgiveness and ask for a release of that situation.

Prayers:

Dear God,

I choose to forgive all those who have rejected me until this present day.

I specially forgive _____. for._____.
(Mention those who have hurt you).

When this happened (mention the situation), I felt rejected. (Lord, please) heal my heart and take away the pain.

Dear God,

In response to my pain, I found ways to cope that have caused me more harm.

Please, forgive me in any way that I have inflicted hurt and pain on myself and others.

Please break those bondages now and remove evil attachments.

Show me new ways to cope when I feel let down.

Dear God,

I can see that some of my struggles are due to the pain of rejection.

Please help me become free.

Please forgive me for anything I have done that was wrong and help me to change

Freedom From The Past

Prayer

- I pray for the man or the woman hiding in their cave of fear and disappointment, hurt, betrayal of friend or partner; fear of stepping out, fear of the unknown, fear of the future. I pray you will bring them freedom in Jesus name.

- I pray for men and women who are struggling with unforgiveness and bitterness; those struggling with difficulty in letting go because it is too painful. They repeat the situation repeatedly in their minds like a vicious cycle. I bring a close to that cycle of defeat right now over their minds, in the name of Jesus.

- I pray for men and women struggling with grief, hurt, divorce, bankruptcy, depression, despondency, and disappointment. I pray Jesus will bring you peace! As you do not know how to let go of the brokenness inside, I pray you will grieve and receive comfort, encouragement, and support from others. In the name of Jesus.

- I pray for men and women struggling with guilt, shame, addictions to alcohol, drugs, sex, porn and masturbation. I pray for those trapped in these thoughts and feelings and fearing to tell or face the truth. I pray you will receive help in the name of Jesus.

- **The first main step to freedom is making Jesus Christ your saviour, will you pray with me now?**
  "Jesus, I come to you a sinner. I repent of all my sins and ask you to forgive me and cleanse me by your blood. I now make you the Lord of my life."

Decide To Stop Hiding!

1   Remember to be honest with yourself about your anger and hurt and allow the damage to be assessed by getting help.

2   Decide, you must make a conscious decision to forgive your offenders.

3   Express your pain and responsibility for your actions because of what happened.

4   It is time to stop being the victim and blaming yourself or others. It is time for you to receive help.

5   Focus on the present as you cannot change the past. You can only change your future.

Confession And Affirmations

Remember to speak and confess positive things over yourself to change your inward narratives:

I am more than a conqueror

I am a victor and not a victim

I am fearfully and wonderfully made

I am blessed and focused

I am strong and confident

I am secure

I am enough

I am free and whole

I am healthy

I make wise decisions

I am qualified, empowered, accepted and approved

I am talented

I am fulfilling my destiny

I am highly proactive

I am courageous

I am rising above every obstacle

I am talented and gifted with special qualities

I am patient

I am preparing for the next level

I don't fear man

I don't shy away from change

I don't give up easily

Conclusion

The principles I have shared in this book will enable you to look at your own life and childhood to learn to be honest and open if you have gone through experiences of rejection, abuse, neglect, trauma or always keep secrets and trust no one.

I have written this book so you can realise there is hope, which was promised to you as a seed of hope from birth to give you a drive to reach out for your ambitions and goals. My grandmother would always pray for me and my sisters. Her home was a haven for me as a child.

She gave me a poem when I was a child at 8 years old. The poem read; "An aim in life is the only fortune worth finding, and it is not to be found in foreign lands, but in the heart itself." *By Robert Louis Stevenson.*

Therefore, it is important to reflect on memories from our childhood, which helped mould and shape our mindsets; they helped establish our attitudes and behaviour we have carried for years.

Some of us have lost touch with our natural drive and desires for life. This has prevented us from achieving our end goals.

So as children where we needed to be nurtured and encouraged in our hope and dreams, but unfortunately some of us were not, so our hope and dreams were destroyed and we were driven to live in the cave, cage and the grave (CCG).

Living our lives aimlessly with broken hearts and broken dreams and our hope deferred or postponed. Thinking even God has passed us by and is not interested.

This book was written so you do not have to suffer in silence anymore, so pay attention and STOP! Hiding.

It is time to walk into freedom, where you have been given the keys to unlock those self- contained prisons. It is time to walk in, to remove the fears of self-doubt and regain your self-worth.

- The question is, do you want to receive healing? If so, are you ready and willing to do what's necessary to receive it?
- *He heals the broken-hearted and bandages their wounds. Psalm 147:3 (NLT)*

I wrote this book to empower you for wisdom and recovery of hope with the value of insights and the processes downloaded to me, while I was learning how to break strongholds off my mind. I lived this so you can use the knowledge of how to gain your worth and value from Christ and not from others.

I have experienced the liberty, and freedom, so I challenge you now, STOP! What are you hiding from?

Now is the time to stop believing and producing negatives, but it is the time to believe the truth and produce the positives.

'You cannot walk in a positive lifestyle if you hold a negative mindset' *Shirley Roberts*

'I always remember that my circumstances can change, but I do not allow those traumatic experiences of the past to dictate my future.' *Shirley Roberts*

Without Jesus Christ, my own life was destined for failure, but through the resurrection power of God I became destined to win. The keys I learned and put into practice have launched my life into joy and blessings that I never dreamed possible. A testimony of God's amazing grace!

I share this only to boast in the Lord and tell you that God is no respecter of persons. What he has done for me, he will do for you. *Romans 2:11 (KJV)*

Trust God today to help you be true to His word. Trust him to help you overcome your addictions or shortcomings by the power of his Holy Spirit. Obey him with every breath you take and in every move you make. In choosing God's way, you are choosing victory over the darkness of the grave. You will walk free from self-doubt and regain self-worth, so you can rise to your true potential that was deposited in you from birth. It's time to walk in the assignment.

Just believe!

References

1. Cloud, H & Townsnd, J (2004) Boundaries: When to say Yes, How to say No, to Take Control of your life,

Notes

Chapter 2

[1] Tournier, P (1983) Creative Suffering

[2] Beeson, R & Hunsider, RM (2000) The Hidden Price Of Greatness

Chapter 3

3 The Cross and the Switchblade, Film,June 1970, USA. David Wilkerson.

Chapter 4

4 www.healthscopemag.com Toxic Relationships; What they are and 8 Types in health Scope
By Thomas L. Cory, Ph. D.

5 Darling, LW (1985) "What to do about Toxic Mentors" The Mentoring Dimension: The Journal of Nursing Administration, Maypp.43-44.

6 Everydayhealth.com – signs of Co-dependency by Sharon Wegscheider-Cruse

Chapter 5

7 Film (2005) DC Comics

8 Ellen Biros, Licensed Clinical social worker in USA

9 Readers Digest Universal Dictionary (1987) Meaning of Accuse

10 Readers Digest Universal Dictionary (1987) Meaning of Offence

Acknowledgements

First of all I give thanks to God, who has given me the inspiration to write this book and the opportunity to make a difference in the lives of many people.

A special thanks to my immediate family, my husband Ken, my daughter and son-in-law Jessica and Dami, who have all been an immense source of encouragement and strength towards producing this book. I thank God for their lives.

To all my friends and family who reviewed this book at one time or another. I say a big thank you.

I would like to say a big thank you to Florence Igboayaka my sis-in-law and coach for her patience and support in helping me birth this book into existence.

Also I would like to thank my launch team for their amazing work.

Thank you all for buying this book, which I know will remain as a source of help and empowerment in your life!

Printed in Great Britain
by Amazon